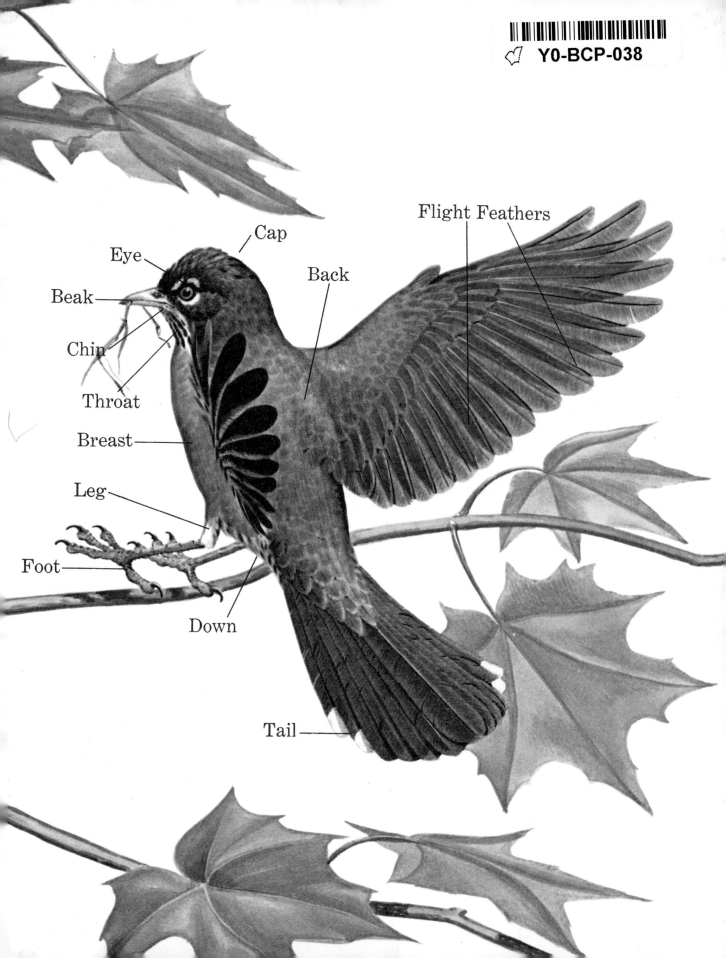

Cap

Eye

Beak

Chin

Throat

Breast

Leg

Foot

Down

Tail

Back

Flight Feathers

Y0-BCP-038

Beginning Knowledge Books are for the young reader who is eager to learn about the world around him. Beautiful color illustrations and simple words are guides that offer a wealth of carefully chosen answers for young questioners. The editors of the Beginning Knowledge Books are grateful for the expert assistance of: Miss Amy Clampitt, Librarian, National Audubon Society, 1952-59; Miss Elaine Fried, Bank Street College of Education; Guy Coheleach, Ornithologist, Takapausha Museum of Natural History.

The Beginning Knowledge Book of
Backyard Birds

by Hanniford Rush / Illustrated by Guy Coheleach

CARDINAL	EVENING GROSBEAK
ROBIN	JUNCO
BROWN THRASHER	CATBIRD
BALTIMORE ORIOLE	RUBY-THROATED HUMMINGBIRD
TUFTED TITMOUSE	STARLING
BLACK-CAPPED CHICKADEE	RED-HEADED WOODPECKER
BLUE JAY	FLICKER
MOCKINGBIRD	PURPLE GRACKLE
HOUSE WREN	ENGLISH SPARROW

A RUTLEDGE BOOK

prepared and produced for The Macmillan Company
Copyright © 1964 by Rutledge Books, Inc.

Backyard Birds

Birds can be found everywhere in the world. The largest bird, the ostrich, is taller than most men. The smallest, a hummingbird, 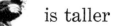 is not much bigger than two of your fingers.

A bird is the only living creature with feathers. Body feathers are small and have soft patches called "down." These body feathers keep the bird warm. Flight feathers 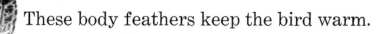 are longer and stiffer than body feathers. They help the bird fly.

Most birds grow new feathers and shed their old ones once a year. When a feather drops from one wing, another falls from the other wing.

How can you learn to tell one bird from another?

A bird's feathers are the first things you notice.

What color is the bird? Has it a bright yellow

breast like the meadowlark?   Has it bands

of color across its tail feathers like a waxwing?

A bird's wings tell something else about it.

Does it have very large and strong wings like the

eagle's?   Then it must do a great deal of

flying. Does it have short and broad wings? Then it

lives close to the ground. Most backyard birds

fly often, but not for long distances.

Nearly all birds build nests.   Nests keep

birds' eggs safe. Later the nest is a cradle for

the small birds, after they hatch from the eggs.

What do birds eat? Look at a bird's bill.

Is it short and thick like a goldfinch's?

That bill is used for cracking hard seeds. Is it a middle-size bill like a tanager's? Then the bird probably eats insects. Owls and hawks have sharp hooks on the ends of their bills. They eat meat. Those hooks help them tear up their food. Birds must eat lots of food all day long to stay alive. This is why a feeding station will bring so many birds to your backyard.

A bird's feet and legs can tell you a lot about it. Some birds have long, thin legs like a sandpiper's. They live near water and do a lot of wading. Or perhaps a bird's feet have sharp, curved claws, like a hawk's. Then it must be a bird who swoops down and picks up its food with its feet. Are its feet webbed like a duck's? If they are, it spends much of its time swimming or floating on the water.

Most of the backyard birds in this book are perching birds. They have three toes pointing forward and one toe pointing backward. These feet make it easy for the bird to get a good grip on tree branches.

Two birds in this book, the flicker and the red-headed woodpecker, are climbing birds. They have two toes pointing forward and two pointing backward. With these special feet, they can climb straight up and down tree trunks.

The backyard birds in this book live near people's houses. They build their nests in nearby trees or bushes or in birdhouses.

Look closely when next you see a flash of wings. Which backyard bird do you see?

Cardinal

The eggs are blue-white and have spots. They are about 1 inch long.

The cardinal's nest is woven of tiny branches and dry grass.

Bright red, wearing a black mask on his face—that is the cardinal.

The cardinal does not go South for the winter. It stays at home through snow and cold. Other birds choose a new mate every year. But cardinals keep their mates for life.

Cardinals live in low bushes and vines. Do not look for them high up in the trees.

The cardinal's thick, broad bill shows that it likes to eat seeds. But it also eats worms, caterpillars, and grasshoppers.

Every spring, the cardinal and its mate look for a safe place to build their nest. The cardinal finds seeds for its mate. They sing to each other. The cardinal's mate is also beautiful, although her feathers are not as bright. Each year they raise another family.

The cardinal is about 8 inches
long. He has bright red feathers.
The female has duller colors.

Robin

The female robin is not as bright-colored as the male. She lays 3 to 5 lovely blue eggs.

Everyone recognizes the robin—its orange-red breast, its lively hop, the way it hunts worms.

The robin seems to like people, too. Most robins live in parks and in backyards. They are most often seen on the ground or on low branches.

The robin works hard to help raise its family. It feeds its mate while she sits on the eggs. Later, they both bring food back to the little birds. The male will fight bravely to protect its family.

Brown Thrasher

Brown thrashers, mockingbirds, and catbirds are part of a family called "mimic thrushes." All three are slim and handsome birds. All have long tails and slightly curved beaks. And all three have beautiful voices.

The thrasher goes South for the winter and returns North in spring. It prefers to live in the woods, but it is often seen in city parks. It likes to perch on the tops of small trees and to sing away.

Nearly half the brown thrasher's length is tail. Its back is red-brown. The eggs are pale blue with tan spots.

Baltimore Oriole

Oriole eggs, gray with dark marks, are less than 1 inch long.

The orioles' nest is like a bag about 6 inches deep.

Baltimore orioles are famous for two things — their bright color and their nest, which looks like a bag.

The orioles fly South in winter. When they fly North, in April or May, they look for a nesting place. They will settle for an apple tree or maple. But what they like best is an elm. Elm trees have swinging branches which are good for the kind of nest orioles build.

When they have found a branch with a fork in it, the orioles drop bits of string, grass, and moss over the forked place until they have built up a big pile. More bits are woven in to make it strong. The female oriole may hang upside down as she works.

The nest is lined with moss. And then the oriole can lay her eggs in a home that swings gently back and forth, like a baby's cradle.

Baltimore orioles are 7½ inches
long and eat insects. Only
the male is orange and black.

Tufted Titmouse

The tufted titmouse has a gray back, white breast, brown patches on the sides. It lays white eggs in tree holes.

From the snowy woods comes a happy call that sounds like "Peter… Peter!" It is the tufted titmouse, telling the world that ice and snow don't bother it.

Titmice travel in groups. They swing, head down, from telephone wires or tree branches. They chase one another and chatter all the time. They gather at feeding stations.

The tufted titmouse likes woods. But it sometimes builds its nest in tree holes near houses.

Black-Capped Chickadee

The black-capped chickadee, like its cousin, the tufted titmouse, does not fly South in the winter.

The chickadee is bold. Often it is first to come to a new feeding station. It is not afraid of people and can often be taught to eat from a hand. "Dee, dee, dee!" it calls.

The chickadee will dig a nest if it has to. But it much prefers to nest in a tree hole dug by some other bird.

Chickadee eggs are white with pretty brown dots.

The black-capped chickadee is 5 inches long. It wears a black cap and bib. It nests in tree holes.

Blue Jay

The jay's inch-long eggs are green or tan with brown spots.

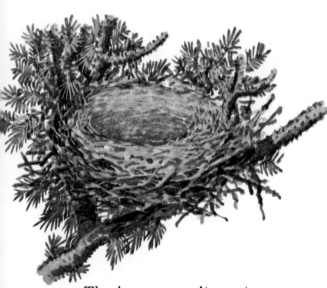

The jay weaves its nest of sticks and soft grass.

The blue jay often appears at backyard feeding stations. The jay is a fairly big bird. When it arrives, small birds usually fly away.

The blue jay is comfortable in any weather. It is found North and South, winter and summer. It may fly very high, or close to the ground. When it can, it lives near oak trees, for they give it acorns in the winter when insects are hard to find.

The blue jay is good to its family. In spring, when it is time for the eggs to be laid, it builds a nest high up in a tree and hides it well. Few people ever see a jay's nest.

The blue jay's loud cry is not a pretty sound. But other birds listen for it. Its angry "Haw . . . haw . . . haw!" often warns the other birds that an enemy is on the hunt in their neighborhood.

Blue jays are about 1 foot
long. Male and female
have the same coloring.

Mockingbird

The mockingbird is gray and white, 10 inches long. It always looks neat, but its nest does not.

Not many birds can sing as well as the mockingbird.

But the mockingbird gets its name from another talent. It can make itself sound like a woodpecker, a blue jay, a cardinal. It can pop like a cork or buzz like a saw. It can imitate a barking dog or a clucking hen. Sometimes it sings the songs of other birds.

The mockingbird stays in the South all year round. It likes to sing where human beings can hear.

House Wren

The wren will nest in a tree hole if it has to. But it would rather have a man-made birdhouse. The house must be small. Its door must be no wider than 1¼ inches. The wren likes to keep large birds out.

If there are other birdhouses near, the male wren may fill them all up with sticks.

The house wren – called "Jenny Wren" – talks a lot. It is always in motion. It makes a cheerful and welcome neighbor.

The little wren has a gray-brown back, white stomach, perky tail. Its eggs are the size of jelly beans.

Evening Grosbeak

The grosbeak lays 3 to 4 eggs, blue-green in color.

Grosbeaks make small nests from twigs and roots.

The evening grosbeak spends its summers in Western pine forests. It flies East for the winter.

The grosbeak belongs to the great family of finches. The sparrow, the junco, and house canaries are also finches. Finches are seed-eaters and have short, thick bills. "Grosbeak" means "big beak."

The grosbeaks travel in groups of 5 or more. They gather most often at feeding stations.

The grosbeaks are very fond of sunflower seeds. But they will also eat the seeds of maple, dogwood, pine, and sumac trees, and many kinds of berries. In the summer the grosbeak eats some insects, too.

The evening grosbeak builds its nest in a pine tree. In winter, when it flies East to New England, it is most often seen near evergreens.

The evening grosbeak is 8 inches long. It is yellow with white and black wings. The female is paler.

Slate-Colored Junco

The junco is 6 inches long. Its
nest is a deep cup. It lays
pale green, brown-spotted eggs.

The junco comes to the United States only for the winter. It spends its summers up North, in Canada.

You can recognize the junco by its habits. It is often seen feeding on the ground. The dark gray feathers of the junco are easy to see against snow. When it flies, you can see the pretty white feathers in its tail.

The junco loves the seeds of many weed plants. By eating these seeds, it keeps weeds from spreading.

Catbird

The catbird gets its name from its voice, which can sound like the *meow* of a cat. It often fools dogs. But it has a beautiful voice and can also sing very sweetly.

The catbird likes to be noticed. It has very little fear of human beings. You can get quite close to it. It will sit within a few feet of someone who is watching. The catbird likes a bush or a low branch. If the person pays no attention, it will often call out, as if saying, "Hey, look at *me!*"

The catbird is dark gray with a rusty patch under its tail. It lays green-blue eggs, about 1 inch long.

Ruby-Throated Hummingbird

Two ½-inch long eggs are laid by the hummingbird.

The nest, small as a quarter, is lined with moss and spider web.

The ruby-throated hummingbird is the smallest bird in the United States. Hummingbirds are only about 3 inches long. Many other birds can fly at great heights or speeds. But hummingbirds can stay in one spot in air and can even fly backwards.

Hummingbirds move their little wings back and forth very fast. Their wings move so fast that they make a humming sound. That is why this bird is called "hummingbird."

The feathers of the ruby-throated hummingbird have a metal-like gleam. This metal-like shine is called "iridescence." Other birds, like the starling and grackle, have iridescent feathers, too.

The ruby-throated hummingbird pokes into flowers with its long beak, searching for nectar and insects to eat. It likes trumpet flowers best.

The tiny bird needs its long bill
to reach into flowers. Only the
male bird has the ruby-red throat.

Starling

The starling is 8 inches long. It will nest in a birdhouse. The eggs are a pretty blue.

The first starlings were brought to New York City from England many years ago. Since then, starlings have spread all over North America.

The starling is a city bird. Many people consider it a noisy pest. It never travels alone. Starlings love to crowd all over public buildings and to fly in large groups.

The starling will nest just about anywhere. Sometimes starlings drive other birds away by taking over their nesting holes.

Red-Headed Woodpecker

The red-headed woodpeckers have the right name. They peck a lot of wood. And red feathers cover their whole head from the shoulders up.

The red-head has a beak like a drill, a tongue that can scoop up food, a tail that is used for support. Like its cousin, the flicker, the red-head gets insects by pecking them out of tree bark. But some it catches on the wing. The red-head is the only woodpecker that can capture insects while it is flying.

The red-headed woodpecker is about 10 inches long. Its eggs are white. It often nests in telephone poles.

Flicker

The flicker lays 6 to 8 white eggs, 1 inch long.

Flickers prefer trees, but will nest in poles or posts.

When the flicker sits with folded wings, it is hard to spot. But when it flies, white feathers above its tail and yellow under its wings "flicker" into sight. That is a good way to remember the name of this bird.

The flicker is a woodpecker. Like others of its family, it has a beak as sharp and hard as a nail. With this beak, the flicker drills holes in trees, looking for insects to eat. When it finds them, it shovels them up with a long, sticky tongue.

Along with beaks like drills and tongues like shovels, flickers also have useful tails. These short, stiff tails help to support them against the up-and-down trunks of trees.

The flicker's nest is a hole drilled into a dead tree. As it drills, bits of wood fall inside the hole, making a soft lining for the eggs.

The flicker is a big bird, 13 inches
long. The male has black feathers
above its beak. The female does not.

Purple Grackle

The grackle is big, black, and sleek.
It nests in pine trees, lays
pale-blue eggs with brown spots.

The purple grackle is sometimes mistaken for a starling. Both birds travel in crowds. Both live in cities. Both of them look black, but have feathers that shine with color when the light strikes them.

But the grackle is 12 inches long, much larger than the starling. It is smooth. The starling looks untidy.

Also, the grackle walks. Most birds hop, both feet together. But grackles put one foot in front of the other, as people do.

English Sparrow

The English sparrow can be found in the country, but it prefers city life. It hunts for its food in cracks in sidewalks.

The English sparrow is a member of a family called "weaver finches." It is a distant cousin of the grosbeak and the cardinal. Like them, it has a short bill, for cracking seeds.

The English sparrow, like the starling, was brought here from England and turned loose. It is now a common American bird, as well.

English sparrows are about 6½ inches long. They make nests of grass or trash, lay 5 or 6 gray-spotted eggs.